Friendship Zone for Kids Ages 8-10

*Kids Guide to Making Good Friends and Build
Strong Social Relationships*

By

Teri Dennis
The Readers Library

About the Author

Teri Dennis is a clinical psychologist and author. He has more than twenty years of experience in this field. He has written many books for children. He is an expert in child development and parenting. His main focus has always been on improving people's parenting skills and creating a safe and healthy environment for children.

'Friendship Zone for Kids Ages 8-10' is one of his best works to help children and parents build healthy and constructive social relationships.

Table of contents

ABOUT THE AUTHOR.. 3

A NOTE TO PARENTS... 6

INTRODUCTION.. 8

CHAPTER 1: THE JOY OF HAVING FRIENDS 11

1.1 Alicia, A Friend of All... 11

1.2 Everything Seems Fun 14

1.2 No Need to Be Alone.. 19

1.3 Who Is a Good Friend? 21

CHAPTER 2: WILL YOU BE MY FRIEND? 26

2.1 Show Them You Are Ready to Make Friends 26

2.2 Let's Do This Together.. 34

2.3 Do Not Push 37

CHAPTER 3: NOT ON GOOD TERMS?... 41

3.1 Let's Fight These Tough Times Together 42

3.2 Respect Each Other... 47

3.3 Let Bygones Be Bygones 48

Chapter 4: Say 'No' To Bullying.. 56

4.1 What is Bullying? 56

4.2 Set Boundaries...58

4.3 Be Who You Are 62

CHAPTER 5: MY FRIENDS, MY LIFE! 65

5.1 Know Yourself More Closely 65

5.2 Let's Grow Together 73

5.3 Keep Your Friends Close..75

PUTTING IT ALL TOGETHER 84

A Note to Parents

Making friends comes naturally to certain children, just like a breeze. Simply said, their friends are drawn to them. Many children, however, require further assistance with this critical life skill. Some kids could experience shyness, insecurity, discomfort, or confusion regarding what to say. Making friends is just the start. Finding ways to keep a friendship alive requires techniques to get through both happy and bad situations.

Whether making friends comes naturally to a young child or not, they can all use assistance with social skills for them or something more difficult. Having social skills is a broad concept. Empathy tells us to comprehend another person's feelings, ideas, emotions, and knowledge. It entails consciously placing yourself in someone's situation.

Many other skills can develop when kids keep empathy top of mind. For instance, many people find talking about themselves most engaging and comfortable. Therefore, empathy aids in reminding a person when speaking with a friend or potential friend. When going over specific social skills or engaging in activities with kids, it can be beneficial to encourage children to focus on empathy.

Each chapter in this guide is supported by discussion questions and activities for your kids. Teach your kids that they shouldn't call anybody who did anything harsh or mean by their name. Some kids are more reluctant to interact. A little help may be sufficient to persuade them to cooperate, but do not put them under duress or pressure.

Establish a secure environment for conversation. Do not mock errors or incorrect responses, and distribute appreciation equally among the kids. Discussions in small groups will probably feel fewer shy children may find these less daunting than large-group ones, and they offer more possibilities.

This book is for you, teachers, counselors, and family members. You can assist children how in making and keeping friends, resolving disputes, and getting along better. It can begin building great and long-term friendships for your child.

We encourage you to read this book with your child and discuss the stories, topics, and activities even though it is intended for children to use and enjoy alone. You are in the right position to support children in developing their sense of self-worth and personal power as caring people and friends. Be respectful to them. Encourage them to be the best versions of themselves, but do not demand perfection. Let them take calculated chances and learn from their errors. Give them the chance to decide for themselves. Invite them to express their emotions, aspirations, and needs for the future. Be someone they can confide in and talk to about the things that are important to them.

We hope that the concepts and resources offered here will someday be a standard component of every curriculum, enabling all children to learn how to be themselves and have healthy friendships.

Introduction

What qualities do you value in a good friend? Life is about having deep connections and true friendships. This book is about how to make, retain and cherish good friends. Friendships can make you feel accepted, provide you the chance to share experiences, make you smile and laugh, and make you feel connected. When you need support, friends can be a valuable resource. While some people have no trouble making friends, others occasionally do.

Life is an adventure, and our journey through it is no exception. But sometimes, things go bad. That is where friends come into the picture. If a friend does not show up when they say they would, then feeling angry is normal. But pause and inhale deeply. When you are at ease, express your feelings to the other person.

Find out if they are bothered by anything; perhaps they did not mean to be rude. You may get back on track and make your journey more serene by finding respectful solutions to issues.

You will have the opportunity to read about how other children have formed and maintained friends throughout this book. Consider what makes you unique and what you like about yourself as you go toward learning how to create and keep friends. If you are proud of the things you accomplish, how you act, or your skills, acknowledge it!

As you meet new people, think about the qualities you want them to like about you. After that, consider what friendship means and how you may help someone else. Have you ever considered the reasons behind your desire for friends? Do you understand what you hope to get from a friendship? Many children may think that a good friend will share their hobbies or have similar opinions. They might seek individuals who have a sense of humor and who want to hang out a lot.

It is common to enjoy being alone occasionally. You can sing, dance, read your favorite books, or engage in other hobbies when alone. You do not need to be concerned about what someone else wants to do. If you are ready to resume social interactions, you can get in touch with your buddies. Finding a harmonious balance between alone time and social time with friends is crucial for maintaining your friendships.

Children may be on the same basketball team, living next door to one another, in the same class, or just be the same age. A single factor connects people, but deeper relationships are also necessary for friendships. The foundation of a strong friendship is discovering a wide range of mutual interests and spending time together doing those things!

Finding shared interests like doing science projects, making up songs, dance routines, scrapbooking, playing basketball, or riding bikes will keep kids and their friends at the hip. The commonality between you and your friend will be what initially draws you together. The support and encouragement of parents and teachers of the extra activity will enable kids and their friends to explore their interests, discover activities they enjoy doing together, and assist in cultivating their interests.

Children have a small circle of friends with whom they share specific interests. Angie enjoys playing with her neighbor Sarah and making crafts, whereas Angie and Julia enjoy taking dance courses and creating their routines. Friends do not necessarily have the same interests. We might like doing one thing with one friend and some other activity with another friend.

"Friendship Zone for Kids Ages 8-10" is divided into five chapters. You will become more adept at making friends, resolving conflicts as you go along, and handling bullying. You will learn how to assert yourself politely but firmly so you do not escalate the situation. Throughout the book, you will also find stories and easy activities that will let you examine your life to see how you can apply the concepts you are reading about to everyday situations.

You will get more from the book if you practice the suggested activities. As you read, keep a notebook nearby so you can finish the activities, write down your thoughts, and make notes. Your writing is for you alone. You are not required to share it with anybody else. Make sure to discuss and practice some of the exercises with other children and adults.

You will increase your self-assurance in interacting with others in this way. Additionally, you will improve your ability to express yourself in a courageous, powerful, courteous, and honest manner. You can always choose how you define a friendship, how much free time you would like to spend with friends, and what sorts of activities you might enjoy doing with others in this book. Good luck in establishing, maintaining, and cherishing your connections!

Chapter 1: The Joy of Having Friends

In this chapter, you will learn:

- Who is a friend?
- Why does everything seem fun with friends? and
- What are the characteristics of a good friend?

1.1 Alicia, A Friend of All

Alicia was a popular student at her high school. She was witty and amusing, and she got along with everyone. It was not by chance that she was so well-liked. She has tried to be kind and friendly to everyone since she was a child. She used to invite the entire class to her birthday celebration. She would also give everyone gifts from time to time. She rarely had the opportunity to spend time with any of them individually. However, she considered herself quite fortunate; no other girl had as many friends at school and in the area.

One day, however, everything changed. Everyone was having a great time at school that day, painting, distributing gifts, and drawing. Everyone was required to prepare three gifts for their three closest friends that day in class. Alicia relished the opportunity to pick three fellows among the dozens she had.

On the other hand, Alicia was the only one who had not received a present after all the gifts had been created and distributed among classmates! She was devastated and cried for hours. After working to create so many friends, no one thought of her as their best friend. For a while, everyone came over and attempted to console her. Each of them, however, only stayed for a brief time before departing.

She realized she had been a good friend to many kids but had not been a true friend to any of them. She had tried not to dispute with anyone and to pay attention to everyone, but she had discovered that those efforts were insufficient to form a meaningful friendship.

Alicia asked her mother where she could find true friends when she returned home that night, having caused quite a puddle with her tears. 'If you truly desire sincere friends, you must devote real-time affection to them. You must always be available to a loyal friend in good and terrible times.'

'However, I aspire to be everyone's buddy! I need to divide my time among all of you! 'Alicia retorted.

'My dear, you are a great girl,' her mother observed, 'but you cannot be everyone's best friend.' Because there is not enough time available to everyone, having only a few true pals is conceivable. The others will be acquaintances or playmates, but not close friends.'

Hearing this, Alicia resolved to amend her behavior to make some true friends. She pondered what she could do to make true friends. She remembered her mother's advice. Her mother was always willing to assist her. She tolerated Alicia's dislikes and troubles, forgave her, and adored her.

That is how you make friends!

Kindness is defined by impact, not the intent. Sometimes you get carried away with hugging and kissing a classmate, or you insist that another child has to play only with them. It does not count as kindness if the other child feels uncomfortable with this behavior. You may need to find less intrusive ways to express liking.

Who is A Friend?

We all have distinct qualities that we seek in a friend. A few things that many people value are listed below. You are bound to come up with more suggestions to add to the list.

A friend is someone with whom you can try some things like:

- Play
- Hang out
- Explore
- Tell stories
- Exchange news
- Laugh
- Cry, and
- Discover new things

A friend is someone from whom you can learn new things; rely on when you have difficulty, and support when you have a problem.

Friendships are not just enjoyable, beneficial, and dependable. They're also beneficial to your health! People with friends are more likely to: be happier, achieve better in school, be more successful in their adult lives, be healthier, and live longer.

Yes, you can live longer. Is not it incredible? Perhaps, but it is true.

1.2 Everything Seems Fun

Jack's Friendship Story

Like any child, Jack enjoyed playing with toys and games. He used to play with cuddly animals and toy cars while reading books. He frequently played with his imagination, allowing everything around him to vanish. Jack used to feel delighted in that situation.

However, Jack was not always content. He suffered from an uncommon illness. It had an odd name that he could not even say. Few people have the disease, which is rare. He used to experience pain occasionally and was frequently exhausted by it. He rarely ventured outside to play when this used to happen. Even his made-up world seemed uninteresting to him. He used to feel sad and angry as a result. Making new friends was more difficult because of all that.

Jack's parents took him to the hospital. All Jack wanted was to be well enough to play outside with the other kids, but he did not always grasp what the doctors were saying.

Finally, Jack's first day of school arrived. He was eager to make friends and get to know other kids. Jack sat next to Peter, a kid who urged Jack to join him in building a house out of building blocks. Peter and Jack were extremely pleased with the enormously large house. The other kids crowded close to it to gawk at it.

Jack's first day went smoothly. However, it was then time to go outside and play.

Peter exclaimed, "Let's run!"

Jack said, "But I cannot run."

"Oh!" In shock, Peter said.

Peter entered the playground. Jack observed the other kids playing outside from the window.

Jack could not run about with the other kids as the days passed, so he frequently had to stay home alone. He remained silent because he did not want anyone else to hear how miserable this made him feel.

His parents occasionally picked him up from school early to take him to the doctor for checkups. Jack had to skip a friend's birthday celebration because of a doctor's appointment. Jack lost his cool. Not fair, in my opinion!

Some students at the school began complaining that Jack was boring and that they no longer wanted to play with him. Because his mother used to decline any invitation that Jack received from his classmates.

She had remarked, "Why invite him when he does not even play with you?" While the other kids play, all he does is sit in the corner of the room."

Jack's melancholy increased as a result.

Peter further considered Jack's feelings of being abandoned daily during breaks from school when his leg was injured. It was difficult to stay inside, seated, and watch the other kids play and have fun while you were absent. Jack could not play as other kids could, so he realized he did not choose to run with Peter and his pals.

Peter could resume running once his leg had fully recovered after many weeks. He did not, however, forget how depressed he had been while having that injury. He resolved to try to be a good friend to Jack.

It was soon to be Jack's birthday. No one would attend Jack's party, he feared. At school, he noticed that many kids were avoiding him. He was unaware that his friend Peter was planning a surprise for him.

Jack was waiting in the playroom on the day of his party. The only thing missing was the other kids; otherwise, there was juice, cake, and snacks. Jack waited for someone to arrive as he regarded the window. He waited and waited, but nobody showed up.

Jack became depressed and frustrated.

He abruptly heard a loud sound coming from the outside. Peter smashed open the door. All of the other students in the class came after him.

For Jack's birthday, everybody had shown up! They brought different gifts. Together with Jack, they engaged in indoor games.

"Jack enjoys playing games, but he gets quite tired because his body functions differently from ours," Peter explained to the other kids before arriving. Therefore, playing games inside is preferable.

When the other kids got it, they were delighted to join in on the celebration of Jack as well. Jack was thrilled.

Peter frequently sat next to Jack after his birthday celebration at school, and Jack played games with the other kids inside. Even though Jack had to visit the hospital frequently, he no longer experienced classroom loneliness.

In addition to learning how much fun can be had when everyone participates, Jack never forgot the generosity of his schoolmates.

Friendships teach you how to manage, explore, and enjoy your emotions. It is natural to disagree, dispute, get your feelings hurt, and apologize when you make a mistake when you have friends.

Friends must learn to share, take turns, collaborate, and compromise. You are maturing as you discover how to accomplish these things. You are figuring out how to function in the real world. You will be happy in the future if you learn to get along now.

You compare yourself to others when you have friends and manage relationships. You learn much about yourself by seeing what other people think of you. Maybe you do not think you are particularly bright, but a friend thinks that it is interesting how you can disassemble and reassemble things. You might begin to think of yourself as intelligent. Perhaps you make a lot of jokes while you should be listening or working. Your pals enjoy your sense of humor, but they request you to be silent when it is time to concentrate.

Learning how to get along with others can benefit you in various ways. For example, you may do well in school, but if you do not get along with your teachers, coming to school will be much more difficult for you. You could get into big problems if you lose your cool, forgetting that you hurt people's feelings.

Friendships are still vital as you become older. You will want pals who can assist you when you need it, offer you transportation to locations, go to the movies with you, celebrate your birthday, shoot hoops with you, or simply talk to you. Getting along with others is crucial when you are a grown-up and do a job.

With them, everything seems fun. Right?

Group Activity

Speaking with someone is a two-way conversation in which one person speaks while the other listens. Both people, however, use more than their mouths and ears. A listener should watch what a person's face says because it can reveal a lot about their feelings. To learn two-way communication, work in pairs or small groups with other kids and take turns expressing various emotions through facial expressions.

Make flashcards for various emotions, such as sadness, surprise, happiness, worry, excitement, confusion, and nervousness. One kid selects a card randomly and, without revealing the card to others, creates a face that conveys that feeling. The others make guesses as to what it is. Afterward, hand the cards to the next youngster and repeat the process.

1.2 No Need to Be Alone

A friend is someone you know and like. Friends communicate with one another and spend time together. They also assist one another when they are in a bad mood. Friends are persons who can be trusted and looked up to. They are the ones with whom you share your secrets. Friends usually share similar interests. A friend admires a person's abilities and assists or encourages them to make good decisions and stay out of trouble.

The strength of a friendship bond between two persons might differ. They are referred to as best friends if their friendship is really strong. This is frequently accomplished by exhibiting characteristics of friendship, such as being kind, generous, loyal, honest, and having fun. You can fully appreciate the joys of friendship if you have these attributes. In friendship, there are also expectations, demands, and complaints.

If your friends do not meet your expectations, you do not have to abandon the friendship. It all boils down to realizing and assisting them wherever possible. Man cannot survive on his own. He's a social creature. He requires someone with whom he can share his pleasures and sorrows. Friendship is required for both support and sharing.

Getting Along

People are social animals, as you probably know. It is understandable, then, that establishing and keeping friends necessitates "social skills." These are the various abilities that we all employ to get along.

Social skills can be learned. You cannot expect great social skills overnight, just like you cannot expect other super skills.

You must practice. The more you practice, the more proficient you will become.

Friendship also necessitates the ability to examine oneself closely. If you are having problems making friends, consider why. This can be difficult. It requires bravery, but it is worthwhile, and you are capable of doing it. Be truthful to yourself. Perhaps you are shy or lack good social skills. Perhaps you act in ways that make it difficult for others to like you. Some children may be unpleasant, unjust, or cruel. They may lack sportsmanship or have difficulty sharing or taking turns. Some children are excessively rough with one another. Is it you, by any chance?

- If you are unsure what is wrong, ask someone you can trust. Allow yourself to be receptive to what the other person has to say.
- It may be upsetting, but it is an essential first step.
- How else are you going to improve your social skills? You must first determine what you want to work on.
- You should also consider the type of friendships you want. Some children enjoy having a large number of friends. They are quite gregarious and associate with a wide range of people.

Having a circle of friends can be beneficial, but you may feel excluded if it becomes too large. A group of four or five friends would be ideal.

Children want to have a small group of close buddies. Some children have best friends, while others do not. Some children despise being alone, so they spend their spare time with other children. Some people require "alone time" to recharge, so they spend less time with their pals. All of these preferences are perfectly acceptable. Consider what yours is.

What Would You Do in This Situation?

David has his fear of joining in with the other students at school. He tells himself that he does not require the company of others. He convinces himself that he can function without them.

In this chapter, you have discovered a lot of reasons why friends are vital. You have discovered that friends may assist us in various ways and that friendship is a crucial part of growing up. You have discovered that while not everyone is born with the ability to make friends, everyone can improve.

Your Turn

So, if you were David, what would you do?

David would be happy if he could learn to chat with some other kids.

Make up some things he could say to help him accomplish this.

_____

_____

_____

1.3 Who Is a Good Friend?

You will be happier if you have good friends, and being a good friend to others will also make them happy. So, who is a good friend:

You Feel Better When You Have a Good Friend

Friends who are happy for you say and do things that make you feel good, such as complimenting and congratulating you.

Good Friends Help Each Other Out

If you are having a bad day, a good friend will be there for you. If you need assistance, a good friend will try to assist you.

Good Friends Do Not Always Agree on Everything.

Everyone is unique, with unique hobbies and interests. Even if you do not share the same interests, a good friend will support you rather than criticize you for preferring a different band, activity, TV show, or animal! A good friend recognizes that you need to do your own thing and appreciates doing the things you share in common with you.

Good Friend Pays Attention

A good friend lets you talk without interrupting you. They want to hear what you have to say.

Good Friends Do Not Judge

If you tell a good buddy something personal, they will not tell anyone else. You can rely on a good buddy not to judge you. Good friends deal with disagreements courteously and respect each other's boundaries.

You and your friend might disagree on things. You may have said or done something that has irritated your friend. If you inform a good friend that they have wronged you, they will apologize and promise not to do it again.

Friendships Are Mutually Beneficial

It is hardly a good friendship if one of you spends all their time talking and the other spends all their time listening. Instead of one buddy receiving compliments and the other offering them all the time, good friends help each other feel good. You are helping each other feel terrific in a good friendship!

Expand Your Circle of Friendship

Do not restrict yourself to just one "best friend." Your friendship is unique, and you can share it with anyone who needs a friend! Having more than one friend increases your chances of finding someone who can assist you when you need it.

Not Followers, But Friends

You may feel pressured to have many friends and followers in the digital world. Remember that happiness requires only a small circle of friends. It is s a good idea to save your most valuable thoughts and experiences for people who truly care about you.

Your Turn

Here is a little activity for you:

Who, according to you, is a good friend?

_____

_____

_____

How can you indicate that you are listening and interested when talking to someone?

_____

_____

_____

Recall the times when someone aided you in doing something. What made you feel the need for assistance? What did the person do to assist you? How did it make you feel?

_____

_____

_____

Have you ever disagreed with a friend about what game to play, what to watch, or what to do? What steps did you take to resolve the situation?

_____

_____

_____

Have you ever discovered a new TV, game, or activity due to a recommendation from a friend? What was it, exactly? What did you think of it?

_____

_____

_____

Chapter 2: Will You Be My Friend?

In this chapter, you will learn:

- What to do when you try to make someone your friend.
- The fun of playing games and doing activities together.
- Why it is important not to push friendships.

What do you enjoy doing the most? Solving puzzles? Reading books? Riding a bicycle? Playing games? Or watching TV? Whatever it is, what fun it would be to do it with a friend. Playing video games, watching TV, going outside, cracking jokes, and making memories sound double fun when a friend joins. You have already started to imagine that, right?

It is not only about having a good time. When you are down, friends can help you. They can assist you in remembering what you are good at and help you improve in other areas. Friends assist one another, defend one another, and listen to one another. Friends hang out and do nothing together, play together, and enjoy themselves. Sure, friends fight from time to time, but they eventually reconcile, and their friendship has a chance to become stronger than before.

What are your thoughts? Is it simple for you to make, keep, and be friends? Let's find out how to do that.

2.1 Show Them You Are Ready to Make Friends

Max, a nine years old kid, enjoys recess at school. He brings his playing cards with him and plays along with them. He believes that all of the students at his school are bullies. "I am alright," he thinks. "I do not require the company of others." He feels there is no use in trying if it is not going to work out.

But after a while, he looks over and notices the other youngsters laughing and joking while playing tag. He tries to convince himself that he does not care, but he does. It is not easy to play by yourself all of the time.

What Would You Do in This Situation?

You will get some inspiration from this chapter, and at the end of the chapter, you will have the opportunity to revisit Max's story and write up an ending where he can learn to make friends.

Openness

Every friendship starts with indications that both parties are eager to get to know each other. Therefore, telling someone, you like them and expressing an interest in becoming friends with them constitute the first ingredient in creating friends. You can sometimes ask directly, "Will you be my friend?"

Say 'Hi'

Greeting someone is a very fundamental sign of openness. Children who are shy frequently struggle with this. They usually look away or just murmur in response when a different child says "Hello!" to them. They do this because they are uncomfortable and self-conscious, but they are telling the other youngster, "I do not like you," They do not feel that way, but that is what they are saying.

Making eye contact, grinning genuinely, and speaking loud enough to be heard are all components of a friendly greeting. The greeting is also made more personal by using the other person's name. Congratulations after practicing

Another simple method of expressing willingness to friendship is through compliments. We prefer people who acknowledge our better traits since it feels wonderful to be complimented. Keep it short and sweet. Some examples include "Great shot!" for a basketball player, "I like how you sketched the sky!" for an artist, or "Your scarf is gorgeous!" for a child sporting a new outfit.

Kindness

Another approach to express liking is by small acts of kindness. This can be sharing a lunch treat, reserving a seat, lending a pencil, or carrying something for a classmate. One of the finest ways to start a friendship is with compassion because it tends to inspire similar behavior. Usually, kind youngsters are well-liked, but occasionally, kids try to purchase friends by parting with cash or expensive items. This is unsuccessful. Giving excessively can be a desperate attempt rather than an honest effort to offer friendship.

The first component of friendship is expressing openness. However, it does not ensure that someone will enter through that door. You must extend their friendship invites to kids who are likely to want to come on in if you want to boost the likelihood that a relationship will develop. The second component of friendship formation enters the picture at this point.

It does not guarantee that two kids will become friends just because they attend the same school or belong to the same area. Children who you think are similar to you tend to be your buddies. Children also tend to form friendships with kids of different ages, ethnicity, and sex.

Similarity

Therefore, similarity serves as the second component of friendship creation. You feel that you must be so amazing that you attract friends to yourself in the same way that a magnet draws steel. If you say, "You are capable of completing this. You are aware of that! You wish for the admiration of other kids. The message other kids get from you is you consider yourself smarter than others. That is not how you begin a friendship.

A friendship is an alliance of equals. You should look for points of agreement with potential buddies rather than attempting to impress other students.

How Do You Define a Common Ground?

Common ground fosters friendship. Here is a method for comprehending the idea of common ground: Draw two circles that overlap, with one representing you. The second child is in the second circle. Friendships develop in the overlap, the area in the middle. When you talk about anything that does not fall under the overlap, it only applies to you and not to the other child.

How do you ascertain what you share with someone? This is a question you should ask yourself. The best responses can involve keeping an eye on the other kid, getting to know them better, or engaging in activities together to exchange experiences. You do not have to copy everyone else to find common ground. It also does not imply that you cannot make friends with others with different hobbies or backgrounds. It just entails realizing that connections and similarities are the foundation of friendships.

Assume that friendship is unlocked by openness and that compatibility indicates who is most likely to enter it. The third component of friendship building is then what persuades individuals to sit down and stay for a while so that friendships might develop.

Shared fun

Shared enjoyment fosters friendship. To have enjoyment with a friend, you should act in ways that the other kid finds enjoyable, talk about tastes and preferences, and try to prevent or settle arguments.

Become a Good Host

The best thing you can do for your child is to assist them in setting up a face-to-face, activity-based meetup once they have developed a strong bond with another child. You should practice being a gracious host before the playdate. The enjoyment of the guests is the responsibility of competent hosts. They try to respect the guest's wishes and avoid conflict. They also stick close to the guest rather than talking to others or leaving the guest alone.

When you first ask, there could be an awkward pause. You ask a kid, "So, what would you like to do?" and he responds, "I do not know. What are your plans?" You must decide what to do in advance to avoid this. You can choose to start by providing the visitor a choice between two activities when they arrive.

Another choice when setting up the play date is to mention the activity in the invitation. You may invite the other youngster over to bake cookies, play basketball, go bowling, ride bikes, or watch a movie. The other youngster will link you with enjoyment if the joint activity is enjoyable, which encourages them to become friends.

Interesting Question

You must learn to enter a group of children who are already playing and invite others to play with you. Learning to say hello and smile when you meet another child, giving praises, and being polite may seem self-evident that you are ready to make friends.

Here are some questions you can ask other kids with whom you want to make friends:

- What is your favorite school subject?
- What is your favorite dessert?
- Which of your pets is/was your favorite?
- What do you like to do during your summer vacation?
- Do you have a favorite TV show or movie?
- Do you prefer to get up early on weekends or sleep in?
- Which foreign country do you want to visit the most, and why?
- What superpower do you like to have?
- Describe the worst haircut you have ever had.
- Give a brief description of your best friend.
- What would you miss the most if you had to leave your current school?
- What would you like to be known for if you could be famous for anything?

- What would your ideal school day be like?
- What would you like to change about your life?
- What is your favorite after-school activity?
- What is your favorite restaurant, and what is your favorite dish to order there?
- What is your favorite piece of music?
- Which holiday is your favorite and why?
- Who is your favorite teacher, and why?
- What would you do with a lot of money and could do whatever you wanted with it?
- Tell us about a time when you were hurt (e.g., broke a bone).
- What is the most memorable gift or present you have ever received, and why?
- Consider your most cherished wish or dream. What is your biggest roadblock to making it a reality?
- How would you describe your worst day at school?
- What would you choose as the one aspect of your life that you would never change?
- Describe one aspect of your parents/family that you admire and one aspect that you despise.
- Tell me about one thing you admire about me.
- What would you make a TV show or YouTube video on if you could make anything you wanted and know millions of people would watch?
- Is there anything you wish you were more skilled at?
- What concerns you the most when you consider the future?
- What do you believe your friends admire about you the most?

- What do you think we would like to do together if we become friends?

Fun Time!

Here are some games and activities you can do:

Participate in Games

Play role-playing games to learn how to join a game. Pretend you are a member of a group of kids who are having fun, and show them how to join in by asking, "What are you playing?" Rather than asking, "Can I play with you?" which may result in a hasty "no," ask, "How can I join the game?"

Let's talk about nonverbal communication. What was the expression on my face when I asked?

Read Stories about Friendship

Reading stories about making friends or characters from stories about making friends is fun. Discuss what the characters in the stories say and do to resolve their friendship issues and how you can solve them.

Puppets and Role-playing

Face expressions, body language, and phrases that attract or repel friendship can all be demonstrated through role play. Discuss what the person's face looked like and how their voice sounded. Did they make the other kids want to be friends with them?

Role-playing games can also help to foster relationships. Demonstrate positive activities such as smiling and sharing and how those actions make you feel.

Participate in Activities

Smaller groups of children for activities can be less daunting for some children. If you appear shy, talk to another child with whom you are more at ease.

Learn Each Other's Names by Playing Games

We do not rapidly learn each other's names. Make a name book for your class but try to remember them afterwards.

Do Not Be Judgmental

People have different moods during different times of the day. Children say that they are no longer buddies if a friend from yesterday refuses to share a toy today. You must understand that all friends make mistakes and that friends do not always agree with them or do what they want.

Max's Story

It is your turn to suggest to Max that he can try to be open and make friends.

2.2 Let's Do This Together

Humans are "social creatures," as the saying goes. That means we have an innate need to be social—to get to know one another and form bonds. We have lived in communities from the dawn of human history. We look after one another and keep good company. We are in love with our fellows.

It is in our nature to be happier when we are together, at least sometimes, from the minute we are born. Our family provides us with some of that companionship. But we also form essential bonds with others, such as our friends. So, let's do some things with other kids you want to be friends with.

The Good Friend List

This is a simple, straightforward activity in which you are advised to list characteristics that make a good buddy. For example, someone who shares toys does not yell, and so on. Perform this activity with other kids. It would be more fun.

Matching Exercises

Play a game with other kids where one has marble and is required to locate other children with the same color stone. They then join arms and remain together until all groups have been formed. This is a fantastic method to come close to other kids and emphasize the idea that different people can share common interests.

It is Me. It is Me

One kid takes the stage in front of the group and reveals a personal tidbit, such as their favorite animal or color. "That is me!" exclaims everyone else who shares that favorite thing. This game is popular among children since it is interactive. You get to talk about your favorite things, it is entertaining to guess what others will say, and there is yelling.

It is a win-win situation for everyone.

The Land Rover

This is a traditional game that helps you learn your peers' names. You will practice working together by holding hands and attempting to prevent the other from breaking through.

This also provides an incentive for kids to get up and move around.

The Game of Giving Compliments

This game can be played in a variety of ways. You can sit in a circle and toss a beanbag to one another, or they can just name the person who will take their turn next. Regardless, the goal is for each child to have an opportunity to complement a classmate. This teaches children how to give praises and how great it is to be complimented. It also assists a group of children in getting to know one another and grow closer.

On the Same Page

This game is an excellent way to break down walls. Form a small group, ideally with a mix of children with whom you are not already friendly. The group must then come up with things in common. Children learn a lot about one another and discover that they have more in common with children from various social groups than they previously assumed.

Face-to-Face

It challenges children to recognize moods based on facial expressions. Groups must identify what they believe that person is feeling by cutting faces out of magazines or printing out photographs and sorting the faces into heaps based on different emotions. The conversation will be fascinating if the expression is more sophisticated.

Make a call

This popular children's game imparts a valuable lesson about gossip. The children are seated in a circle. The first youngster chooses a sentence or phrase to whisper around the circle. When the final youngster finishes the statement, the entire group chuckles at how dramatically the wording has changed.

Even the most basic information can become messy and distorted as it is passed from one person to the next. This teaches children not to believe everything they hear and seek the truth by going to the source.

2.3 Do Not Push

Let's hear Emily's Story:

Emily's Story of Friendship

Maggie has not responded despite Emily's repeated messages to her over the past hour. She is afraid Maggie has ended the friendship. Maggie revealed to Emily last week that she and Gracey had been video talking frequently. She thought that was why Maggie was not responding to texts which made Emily sad.

Be careful not to see a communication sent to a friend as a test of the friendship.

When Maggie does not answer, though, what should Emily do? Before moving on to that, we need to discuss what she should not do. A friend may find it annoying or overwhelming if you send them numerous messages. It resembles a one-sided water balloon fight in which you are the only one tossing the balls while your friend simply stands there dodging them. The friend finds that to be unfun.

Friends should communicate more like in a game of catch when each takes turns sending and receiving messages. You should step back if you discover that you are sending far more messages than your friend is to make things more equitable.

Emily should also refrain from deciding to never communicate with Maggie again because she did not react. Emily will be rejecting a friend for not doing exactly what she wants if she ends the friendship just out of frustration. That is unkind. It also is not a good justification to call off a friendship like this.

Space is Necessary

Emily must strike a balance between pressuring Maggie for a response and ditching her. She needs to realize that Maggie cannot or does not want to talk for whatever reason. It is alright. When necessary, good friends are willing to give each other space.

Emily should give it a day or two and then make touch with her once more.

While waiting can be difficult, doing so allows Maggie to contact Emily. Despite the momentary lack of response, they can stay good friends as they have been in the past. A good friendship must not end because of a minor hiccup in communication. It is unfair for a friend to say, "If they take too long to reply, that suggests they do not care about me at all." It overburdens the friend and gives small deeds too much significance.

It is crucial to have reasonable expectations for your friends' reactions. Of course, you want a response right away when you are alone at home! However, it can take days or weeks to hear back from certain pals. The friend could not reply at all if the communication were not urgent. It is disappointing, but it may have nothing to do with the friend's opinion of you.

Try to Understand Her Reasons

If Emily is aware that she offended Maggie in any way, she should immediately apologize. That is an effective first step in reconciling with a friend after a disagreement. What if there was not a dispute, though?

Emily must exercise caution when drawing inferences regarding Maggie's lack of response to her communications. She can be making herself miserable unnecessarily if she assumes that it is because Maggie does not like her.

There are many reasons why a buddy might not answer right away. These are a few of those explanations.

- She can be preoccupied with homework.
- Perhaps she has got into some problem.
- Perhaps she is engaging in family activity.
- Maybe she has left her device in the other room, so she does not have it with her.
- Perhaps she failed to charge her gadget.
- Perhaps she is ill and not in the mood to talk.
- She might be taking a break because she is sick of being online.
- She may dislike internet communications and have a poor response rate.

You can take it less personally by considering all the possible reasons a friend can stay silent. Nobody is always available. Thus, it is neither fair nor kind to assume that your friend does not care about you if they do not respond. Just do not push.

Chapter 3: Not on Good Terms?

In this chapter, you will learn:

- How to be together during tough times.
- How to respect each other even if you do not get along.
- Leaving your past behind and being friends again.

Mandy and Joy had not spoken for a long time. It all started when Anne joined them for lunch the other day. Normally, it was just Mandy and Joy. On the other hand, Mandy kept talking to Anne and ignoring Joy that day. Joy was feeling completely excluded. She went to another room. When Mandy spotted her in the other room later, she became enraged and accused her of abandoning her! They had not been speaking for three days then.

What Sparked All This?

Joy desired alone time with Mandy, but Mandy insisted on including Anne. Their desires collided, sentiments were injured, and confrontation happened.

Conflict is frequently caused by hurting someone's feelings. You have probably been in circumstances where someone says or does something that hurts your feelings, either accidentally or on purpose. As a result, you retaliate by saying something harsh or talking behind the person's back.

So, what is Next?

After the person reacts to what you do, what happens next? You have figured it out. Being on bad terms or not getting along with a friend is normal and natural, and it occurs when people hold opposing viewpoints or needs. You want to play basketball, while your friend wants to play video games. Your closest companion wants to talk on the phone; you have a test to prepare for. The issue is not with the disagreement. It is how you handle it. It isn't very pleasant when someone opposes you or instructs you to do something you do not want to do. However, there is one aspect you should know:

When it relates to conflict, you always have the option of how to handle it. You are going to take care of it. This indicates that you wield a great deal of power because your actions will impact the outcome of the conflict.

Many people decide to handle confrontation in unpleasant ways—actions that harm themselves and others. We argue, make sarcastic remarks, call each other names, engage in other forms of cruelty, or fight. All of these factors are negative options.

You can resolve problems in ways that make you happy. And if you follow the advice in this chapter, you will be OK. You will notice that you are getting along better with your friends and other people in your life regularly.

3.1 Let's Fight These Tough Times Together

True friends support you in good and bad times. When friends are unhappy, upset, hurt, terrified, pleased, excited, or celebrating victories, they offer support to one another. Because your friend means a lot to you, a good friend will help through inspiration, kindness, and encouragement.

Celebrate your friend's accomplishment or assist your buddy as much as possible during a difficult moment when a friend has experienced something amazing. So, whenever something unpleasant happens, first of all, try this relaxation technique:

Relaxation Technique

Allow yourself to practice soothing techniques. We typically feel tense and worried when we are angry or irritated. When you disagree with a buddy, you can use these tactics to keep cool. You can practice sitting or lying down in a comfortable position.

Breathing from the belly button. Say something like, "Let's start by breathing normally." As you breathe in and out, pay attention to how your body feels. Next, relax your muscles, place your palm on your stomach, and inhale deeply through your nose until your entire chest and belly are filled with air. Hold your breath for five seconds. Slowly exhale until you are completely out of air. Repeat numerous times until you are relaxed.

Write a Story

Write a short tale or draw a picture depicting two kids in dispute. You must describe the issue and demonstrate how the characters resolve it. Invite your friends to tell their stories to the rest of the class. Encourage writers to explain both of the characters' sentiments in their novel. When the story concludes, how do those feelings change? Instead of writing or drawing their stories, you might create puppets and perform a puppet performance.

Find the Reason

Understanding what irritates or disturbs you and what you can do instead of reacting is one technique to help yourself handle conflicts better. It is similar to preventing a cold or fever. Knowing what makes your body strong — like eating well, getting enough rest, and exercising regularly — may help prevent a cold.

It is worth writing about.

Write about all the possible reasons and use it to learn more about the things that cause you to fight. Observe the situations that frequently cause you to have disputes throughout the next few days. Make a list of these on your form and see what you come up with. Do similar things irritate you?

Understanding what causes your disputes and what works to calm you down might help you avoid situations that spiral out of control. What is the advantage? A happier, even healthier life — researchers have discovered that getting along with others keeps people healthier.

You might be thinking something like this right now:

You are correct. It is not always easy to resolve disagreements. But it is always worthwhile to put up the effort. It is similar to learning to ride a bike. Remember the first time you rode without the aid of training wheels or a firm hand to keep you balanced? In the beginning, you undoubtedly fell and scraped your legs a lot. However, as you got trained, you began to glide with increasing ease.

That was perseverance. You continued trying and persevering until you succeeded. Perseverance is also required while resolving problems — also as bravery. Taking the initiative in resolving a quarrel can feel hazardous. Anything that requires us to change can be frightening at first, but we all have reserves of courage that we've never tapped into. We become stronger through flexing our courage muscles. Are you prepared to flex your muscles? If you are, you have already made the right decision.

Read Children's Friendship Stories

You can find yourself and explore your identities through friendships. Reading friendship story books allows children to maintain and form new friendships. By reading stories about friendship, you can learn to cherish friends and develop positive traits that help you become better individuals. For instance, you become aware of the value of supporting your friends because friends frequently lend a hand in overcoming challenges in life.

Friendship stories often talk about both happy and unhappy times spent with friends. You can then seek answers for any issues in your friendships. In the long run, this makes you happier and helps you preserve your self-worth.

After Reading the Story

Answer the following questions to comprehend the story. Here are a few ideas:

- Who are the characters?
- What are their traits?
- How did they behave? And why?
- Which part of the story do you like the most?
- Which character best resonates with you, and why?
- What would have been your response?

- What did you learn from this?

Give yourself time to consider their answers. You may find it interesting.

Had a Disagreement?

Consider a time when you disagreed with a friend. What went wrong, and how did it turn out?

_____

_____

_____

How does it feel when a dispute is resolved unpleasantly?

_____

_____

_____

Why do you believe it is sometimes difficult for people to apologize?

_____

_____

_____

What would you do if you had to make amends with your friend?

_____

_____

3.2 Respect Each Other

True friends can rise beyond conflicts and talk about their problems with each other. Most importantly, they treat each other respectfully how they'd prefer to be treated. In each of these instances, select the option for the action that a true friend would do.

What Would You Do?

You learn that one of your close friends has made a disparaging remark about you to someone else.

- You rush over and tell her she is no longer your friend.
- Approach your pal and inquire whether or not she has said it. Then tell her you are sorry for hurting her feelings.

You know your entire class has been invited to your friend's birthday except for you. You would:

- Throw a wild party and leave him out. You leave him out because he left you out.
- Pretend you did not want to go to his dull party in the first place.
- Inquire if there was a blunder. Try to figure out what is going on if he did not invite you on purpose.

Today, your friend was quite disrespectful. She spoke in a threatening tone and refused to share during recess. You would:

- Consider how pleasant she is in general. Inquire if she is having a difficult day or something is bothering her.

- Forget about her. Nobody ever treats you like that.
- Go around to all your friends and tell them how rude she was.

3.3 Let Bygones Be Bygones

Let's hear the story of Jacob and Sophia:

It is All Because of Sophia

Jacob: Sophia, my younger sister, drives me insane. She always enters my room without knocking, and when I urge her to leave, she continues to bother me and refuses to go. I chase her, and she keeps screaming all over the place. I wrestle her to the ground after catching her. She tends to cry at times. My mother then screams at me, and then I am reprimanded. Sophia is to blame for everything. She has no right to come into my room! Why should I bother trying to figure it out? She is the one who always initiates things. I also enjoy chasing her down and wrestling her down. It is a blast!

Jacob did not bother to talk to her sister about the matter.

Jacob appears to be more interested in prolonging the fight than resolving it, even though he frequently gets himself into difficulty. His unwillingness is a hindrance. Jacob, like many others, refuses to acknowledge or admit his part in sustaining the peace.

Opening your mind is the first step towards resolving the conflict. Jacob is locked in a cycle of getting into fights with his sister and then being punished. His mother starts blaming him whenever there is a problem. Jacob can break free from this harmful habit by accepting responsibility.

Consider that for a moment. Sure, it is amusing to taunt your sister or brother now and again, but isn't it more satisfying to get along with your roommates and not be in constant trouble? Isn't it also good to have the grown-ups in your life trust you? It is difficult to regain trust once you have lost it. However, once you have it, you will feel a lot better about yourself and have the opportunity to gain more independence.

Not Ready to Sort Things Out?

When you refuse to resolve a disagreement, the following things happen:

Blame Game: You have probably heard of the "blame game," in which you accuse someone of causing a problem. That person retaliates by blaming you. No one takes responsibility for the situation, and the battle never ends.

You may find yourself repeating the same battle, and all of this blaming obscures a crucial fact. Both parties are to blame in some manner. Jacob's sister was at fault because she went into his room without asking, but Jacob was also at fault since he chased her down and wrestled her to the ground. What other options do you think he had for dealing with the situation?

Exaggeration: When no one takes the initiative to put an end to the blame game, the disagreement tends to become louder, meaner, and larger. Exaggeration is what it is. What begins as a minor disagreement can quickly escalate into a massive spat in which everyone is involved, and both parties are emotionally or physically harmed.

Ask yourself:

Do you have conflicts daily? At the very least once a day?

_____

_____

_____

Would you like to have fewer conflicts?

_____

_____

_____

More Confrontations: When people refuse to work things out, the worst thing that happens is that they wind up having constant disagreements, making life even more unpleasant. When this happens to you, you will run into someone you have had a problem with in the past or who you might have a problem with in the future. After a while, you will begin to feel like a conflict magnet. That is no way to have a good time!

What are Your Obstacles?

What are the obstacles that prevent you from completing tasks? Take this simple self-test to check if there are any roadblocks in your way:

- I would prefer to stop fighting, but only sometimes.
- I want to prove myself "correct," and the other person is "incorrect."
- I am not weak.

- I am afraid that people will take advantage of me if I compromise.
- I enjoy being on top.
- I am not fond of the other individual.
- I am terrified of making a fool of myself.
- I am too enraged to deal with the situation sensibly.
- I want to vent my frustrations on the other person.
- I want to avenge someone for something they said or did.

Does any of these apply to you? If yes, you should bring a change in yourself. Ask yourself two questions every time you find yourself feeling or thinking something that could prolong a conflict:

- Is it worth it?
- Am I ready to gather the courage to make a change?

Here is the Deal

Holding on to grudges almost guarantees that your issues will not be resolved. When you always have conflicts, a lot of terrible things happen. People start avoiding you. They begin to consider you a troublemaker. You become lonely as a result of the loss of friends. You are chastised and under stress. You soon begin to feel horrible about yourself all of the time.

Your general health may be harmed. You are establishing a lifetime pattern of negative conflict resolution. Is it necessary for this to happen to you? Not. You may feel compelled to blame or attack the other person, but you are not obligated to do so.

You see, you can prevent confrontations from becoming more serious. Someone must take that initial step, and that someone can be you. Even if you believe the other person is more to blame than you, it is still worthwhile to try to solve the problem.

Instead of blaming the other person, the most mature and honest thing you can do is ask yourself how you might be to blame. Then take the first move toward resolving the issue. You will find out exactly how to achieve this very soon.

Your Turn!

Consider someone with whom you frequently disagree. What are the barriers to your willingness to work with this person?

_____

_____

_____

How do you deal with disagreements? What works? What does not work?

_____

_____

_____

Yes, it can be difficult at times, even impossible. It is worth it, though, if you desire closer friendships, better relationships at home and school, and a positive self-image. You will also get the gratification of knowing that you exercised your courage significantly.

What Happens When You Are Willing to Resolve Disputes?

Here's the good news. It is possible to resolve a problem if only one individual is willing.

Here is why:

You act differently when you are willing to work things out than when you are not. Your intellect, like your ears, is wide open. By doing so, you are demonstrating your ability to listen to what someone says and feels. When you are willing to listen, the other person will likely do the same.

Is this something that always works?

It does not happen every time, but you would be shocked how often it does. When you act mean against someone, they often respond by acting mean toward you. "Hey — Mine!" They will begin to calm down if you are at least willing to listen to what they say.

Phillip: That is my notebook, by the way!

Jamie: No, it is not. It is mine.

Phillip: (grabs from his hand) No, it is not. It belongs to me.

Jamie: Please wait a moment. Let's have a conversation about it.

Phillip: There is nothing to discuss. It is my notebook, of course.

You see the problem. Right?

Your Turn!

Have you ever tried to keep a disagreement going?

_____

_____

_____

Why did you do that?

_____

_____

_____

What happened exactly?

_____

_____

_____

How did you feel after that?

_____

_____

_____

What do You Need to Do?

Put your willingness blocks aside the next time you disagree with a friend, a teacher, or a family member. Remind yourself that you have options for resolving the disagreement. Rather than just attempting to get your idea over, take the time to listen. Even if you disagree, keep your mind open for a few moments and let the other person speak. Then request that the person pay attention to you. Express what you need to say courteously.

Allow your body language and facial emotions to convey the respect that you do with your words. Keep your thoughts open as you speak and listen. Instead of focusing on how to get your way, consider how the problem could be resolved.

Then you will have to wait and see what occurs. Is the issue now resolved? What are your thoughts on what you did?

Chapter 4: Say 'No' To Bullying

In this chapter, you will learn:

- What is bullying?
- Setting boundaries to stop bullying.
- The meaning of being who you are as a person

4.1 What is Bullying?

Bullying is a serious issue. It can cause hurt, sickness, fear, loneliness, sadness, and embarrassment in children. Bullies may injure others by hitting, pushing, kicking, teasing, teasing, or scaring them with words.

A bully may say hurtful things about someone, take their belongings, make fun of them, or purposefully exclude a child from the group. Some bullies use threats or coercion to force people to do things they do not want.

Bullying is a serious issue that affects many children. The majority of children claim to have been bullied or teased. Bullying can make children feel terrible, and the stress of dealing with it can make them ill. Bullying can make children desirous of playing outside or attending school. It is difficult to focus on academics when you are anxious about how you will deal with the bully who hangs around near your locker. Bullying can make school a scary environment, resulting in violence and increased stress for everyone.

Olivia's Story

Olivia told her mom that she did not want to go to school. Her

mom wondered about Olivia's behavior. She asked Olivia if there was any problem going on at school. Olivia hesitated to answer. Her mom told her that when she was a kid, she also did not want to go to school because some kids in the school used to call her different names. Olivia immediately took an interest in whatever her mother was saying. She looked up, "Why did they do that?" Her mother sensed that Olivia had been facing the same problem of being bullied at school.

Her mother asked if she had talked to her teacher about it. Olivia replied negatively. Her mother went to school with Olivia and talked to her teacher about the matter. Olivia's teacher decided to hold a class session about bullying awareness. Things got better at school. Olivia was happy that she shared it with her mother and teacher.

Why Do Bullies Act Rudely?

Some bullies look for a way to draw attention to themselves. They may think bullying is a means to gain popularity or obtain what they desire. The majority of bullies attempt to elevate their status. It can make children feel huge and strong when they pick on someone.

Bullies are sometimes aware that what they do or say is hurtful to others. On the other hand, other bullies may not realize how harmful their behavior can be. The majority of bullies are oblivious to or unconcerned about others' emotions.

4.2 Set Boundaries

Bullies typically pick on someone they feel they have control over. They might pick on easily irritated kids or have trouble defending themselves. When they receive a strong response from someone, bullies could start to accept they have the authority they crave. Bullies may target a victim who is better than them or is in some other way different from them. Bullies can also occasionally single out a young person for no obvious cause.

How to Deal with Bullying?

Bullying affects many children, but what should you do if you are being bullied? Our suggestions are divided into two categories: avoiding a confrontation with the bully and what to do if you come face to face with the bully.

Preventing a Bully Confrontation

Do not even consider giving the bully a chance. Avoid the bully as much as possible. Of course, you cannot go into hiding or skip class. If you can avoid that person by taking an alternate path, do so.

Be Strong and Courageous

You are probably not feeling your boldest when you are afraid of another person. However, sometimes simply being brave is enough to deter a bully. What does a bold person look like, and how do they act? "Do not mess with me," you will send the message if you stand tall. When you feel good about yourself, it is simpler to be brave.

Be Comfortable with Yourself

Nobody is flawless, but what can you do to make yourself

look and feel better? Maybe you would like to get in better shape. If that is the case, you might decide to exercise more, watch less TV, and eat better snacks. Perhaps you think you look best when you shower first thing in the morning before going to school. If that is the case, you might consider getting up a bit earlier to be clean and ready for the school day.

Make A Friend

If you want to avoid being bullied, two is better than one. Plan to walk to school, lunch, recess, or anywhere you think you will run into the bully with a friend or two. If a friend is being bullied, offer to do the same. If you notice bullying at your school, speak up to an adult, stand up for the kid being tormented, and urge the bully to stop.

If You Are Bullied, What Should You Do?

Here are the options:

Ignore that Person

If at all possible, try to disregard the bully's threats. Pretend you are not hearing them and swiftly go to a safe location. Bullies are looking for a huge reaction to their taunting and bullying. Acting as if you do not notice or care is the same as giving no response, which may be enough to deter a bully.

Stand for Yourself

Pretend to be brave and self-assured. Say loudly, "No! Stop it!" to the bully. Then get up and walk away, or run if necessary.

Children can also defend one another by ordering a bully to stop taunting or scaring someone else and then walking away together. Say "no!" and walk away if a bully forces you to do anything you do not want to do. If you do what a bully tells you to, the bully will likely continue to bully you. Bullies target children who do not speak out for themselves.

Do Not Retaliate

Do not hit, kick, or shove back when someone bullies you or your pals. Fighting back only makes a bully happy, and it is also dangerous since someone can get wounded. You will almost certainly get into problems. Staying with others, staying safe, and seeking adult assistance are best.

Do not Express Your Emotions

Prepare ahead of time. How do you keep yourself from being enraged or expressing your displeasure? Distract yourself until you are out of the situation and in a secure place where you may express your concerns.

Inform an Adult

It is critical to inform an adult if you are being bullied. Find someone you can confide in and tell them about your situation. Bullying can be stopped by teachers, principals, parents, and lunchroom assistants at school. Bullies may cease bullying as soon as a teacher notices them because they are terrified of being penalized by their parents. Bullying is unacceptable, and it helps if everyone who is bullied or witnesses someone being tormented speaks up.

Bullies: What Happens to Them?

Bullies almost always end up in trouble. If they continue to be cruel and unpleasant, they may find themselves with only a few friends – usually, other youngsters who are just like them. The power they craved vanishes quickly. Other children go on, leaving bullies in their wake.

Some bullies place blame on others. On the other hand, every child has an option in how they act. Some bullies learn that threatening others does not get them the respect they desire. They may have believed that bullying would make them popular, but they quickly discover that other children regard them as troublemakers and losers.

Bullying children can learn to change their ways, which is excellent news. Teachers, counselors, and parents can all be of assistance. Observing children who treat others properly and respectfully can also be beneficial. Bullies can change their ways if they learn to utilize their power for good. Bullies must ultimately decide whether or not to modify their behaviors. Some bullies grow up to be wonderful children. Others are incapable of learning.

However, no one should put up with a bully's tricks. If a bully is bothering you or someone you know, talk to someone you can trust. Bullying makes people uncomfortable, and everyone has the right to feel safe. Tell someone about it, and continue to tell until something is done.

4.3 Be Who You Are

Mike's Story

Mike was having a difficult day in class. Once more, children taunted him, made fun of him, and attempted to disgrace him when the teachers were not looking. He tried to ignore them, but they persisted. He occasionally wanted to punch them all or leave school and never return.

Mike's mother asked about his day that evening.

He said, "I hate going to school! I am sick of being teased. I wish I could stop attending classes."

His mother told him, "You know you cannot quit. You must begin with yourself, be who you are."

Isabel's Story

Isabel's father held her accountable for everything. Her father yelled at her last night when her little brother broke a plate. He told her, "You would have prevented this from happening if you had cleared the table. If you had been paying attention to him as you should if you would pay more attention, as we've already advised."

She later informed her best friend about it in a text message.

She furiously typed, "He accuses me of things I do not even do!"

Her friend replied, "Parents can be so ignorant. Stop allowing him to manipulate you any longer."

John's Story

John is aware of the study hall silence policy. When Smith kicks him beneath the table without cause, he is quietly working on his math and doing his business. John only says, "Man, stop it!" He barely whispers it and does not even say it out loud.

The teacher immediately tells John to stay after school. The teacher commands, "not another word out of you," as John tries to explain.

While doing so, Smith sits there grinning stupidly.

John discusses it with his family over supper.

His father tells him, "You broke a rule. However, it does not seem like you did it deliberately. Your teacher lacked equity. Just be who you are."

Find Out What Is It All About

What does it imply when Mike's mother advises him to stand up for himself? Should he begin misbehaving with the children who misbehave with him? Should he engage them in combat? Should he try to exact revenge on them for ruining his life?

What does it mean when Isabel's friend advises her to be who you are? Should she respond to her father? Should she punish her younger brother for putting her in danger? Should she enter her room and loudly slam the door?

What does it mean when John's father advises him to be who he is? When the teacher asks John to stop talking, should he comply? Should he punch Smith and hope that he speaks as well? Should he complain about the teacher to the principal?

Have you ever been advised to be who you are? You often act in ways that are not consistent with your personality.

Being assertive for yourself does not entail getting even with another person, acting bossily, or saying and doing everything you want whenever you want.

Here is What It Means:

Being who you mean:

- Be true to yourself and know who you are and what you stand for.
- It means being able to speak up for yourself when necessary and doing so.
- It implies that someone always supports you.

You need inner security, a strong sense of self, and personal power if you wish to stand up for yourself and be who you are. You can learn how to gain personal strength through this book. Knowing oneself is a crucial component of having personal power. If you do not know who you are and what matters to you, it is impossible to stand up for yourself.

Chapter 5: My Friends, My Life!

In this chapter, you will learn:

- The joy of growing together with your friends.
- How to keep your friends close?

Friendship is a great part of life. We experience life with friends as we grow up through playing, talking, laughing, and crying. When you reflect on your childhood, there are undoubtedly many instances involving friends that you can recall. You need to acquire certain abilities if you want to create and maintain friendships. You will learn it all in this book, including:

- How do you form bonds?
- How do you come to learn about your friend's emotions?
- How do you forgive?

5.1 Know Yourself More Closely

Let's start with yourself (be creative in your answers):

All About Me

Where do you live?

_____

_____

Your favorite things, color, places, and food.

_____

_____

_____

Your family.

_____

_____

Your friends' names.

_____

_____

Your strengths.

_____

_____

What do you want to become?

_____

_____

Draw a picture of your happy place.

Briefly describe your personality in a paragraph.

_____

_____

_____

All About My Emotions

Things that make me happy.

_____

_____

Things that make me sad

_____

_____

Things I do when I am happy.

_____

_____

My Anger

Everyone experiences moments of anger. Anger might feel explosive within you. Things can make you feel exhausted. Yes, some children yell, smash things, slam doors, and strike a wall or another person.

Be true to yourself.

Things that make me angry.

_____

_____

Things You Can Do to Control Anger

- Engage in physical activity.
- Have fun outside.
- Play with a ball, engage in physical activity, dance, and jump around.
- Talk to someone close. Express to someone what is upsetting you. Express your emotions in words. Say something like, "I get furious when I have to stop watching TV and go to bed," for instance.

How do you handle your anger?

_____

_____

_____

My Fun Time

Things you do to have a fun time.

With yourself:

_____

_____

_____

With your family:

_____

_____

_____

With your friends:

_____

_____

_____

Feeling Left Out

What happened that made you feel left out?

_____

_____

_____

What options do you have?

- Try to change your strategy to fit in the game.
- Try out a different game.
- Consider a solo activity that you can do on your own.

Peer Pressure

- Pay attention to what the other people are asking of you.
- You think it is a good or bad idea. Why?
- What may occur if you choose to join the group?
- What might occur if you refuse to join the group?

My Trust

How would you define trust?

_____

_____

_____

How can you win someone around to your side?

_____

_____

_____

There is a person you do not trust. Why do you not believe this person?

_____

_____

_____

How can you build trust?

_____

_____

_____

Explain how trust helps to form better relationships.

_____

_____

_____

How would you know whether to trust someone or not?

_____

_____

_____

5.2 Let's Grow Together

Friends are not made, according to those who know what friendship is. Friendships frequently begin when two people are at ease and enjoy spending time together. Relationships just happen. Friends are those with whom a friendship is shared.

Jones and Williams Growing Together

Jones and Williams first met at the supermarket where their mothers used to work. Their mothers figured they might like playing together, and they did! That was how Williams and Jones became pals. Williams and Jones have been buddies for a very long time now. Who knows how much time their bond will endure, not Williams, Jones, or even their mothers.

Friends cannot decide how long they'll stay close. This is because friends cannot agree on too many issues regarding their friendship. People keep doing that, so it must be OK to them.

"I suppose we'll be buddies," a friend could say.

If one person says, "I am having a good time, and I hope we always will have it together." It is alright. It is even better if both of the buddies are experiencing the same. Most people are aware of when a friendship began. However, nobody ever really knows the lifespan of a friendship.

Williams, Jones, Andre, Anna, and Maria appear to be very close buddies when people keep seeing them together. But they do not get along with each other. Jones and Williams are pals who enjoy playing chess. Williams and Andre are good pals who enjoy basketball. Andre dislikes playing chess, and Jones dislikes basketball.

William is Andre's favorite friend, and they play together a lot.

Does a friend ever play with other children?

Yes, it does happen frequently. It may occur between friends or another person. That is how friendship works.

A shift in friendship occurs when a friendship no longer feels as natural or enjoyable as it did at first. It frequently happens because the pals are young people who are also learning and growing. A friend might decide to sign up for a soccer team or a chess club. When a family relocates, there are further possibilities. For instance, two buddies might not play together as frequently, and neither one is sure why.

The bond between Jones and Williams ended up being like that. When Williams called Jones to ask whether he could play, Jones frequently responded, "Not today." Their friendship changed. Even mature friendships experience it. That is how a shift in friendship works. Friends will frequently run into one another in their neighborhood during a shift in friendship.

Friends may occasionally run to the grocery store or the theatre, where they chat or joke for a bit. They might cross paths at school and collaborate in the classroom. Jones and Williams occasionally played together on the playground during their shift in friendship, but not as frequently as before. Jones began to play with other children.

A shift in friendship can occasionally feel warm and considerate. A shift in friendship may occasionally be a little unsettling. They do not spend as much time doing activities together in their spare time. Being together now may seem a little awkward until they get used to the shift in friendship because they enjoyed and shared wonderful times while they were friends.

Jones and Williams interact and collaborate at school, but they no longer spend any of their leisure time together. But now again, they are spending more time playing together. They're close pals again because they have accepted that shift in friendship and built a strong bond by finding new common grounds.

Williams and Jones grew together. Jones joined the chess club during the shift in friendship. Williams occasionally played alone at home and played basketball. He also got engaged in a few novel activities. Williams was first prompted to play by Andre.

Williams and Andre have been friends for a while. They are a part of Williams's book club. Even a year ago, they occasionally played together. They are spending more time playing together. They're close pals.

5.3 Keep Your Friends Close

Sophia and Mia were close friends. They had been friends since Sophia moved in next door to Mia during their second grade. When they were getting along, they hung out together every day after school. They were extremely dissimilar individuals. Mia excelled in her academic pursuits, devoured books, and took dancing lessons. On the other hand, Sophia preferred to play soccer, talk to other students at school, and seldom ever sat down long enough to finish a book's chapter.

At the park across the street, Mia and Sophia would frequently play together. They would engage in sports like soccer or tag. They would also engage in crafts, computer games, or manicures. On some days, they could talk for hours without encountering a single issue, while on other days, they just could not agree.

"The past three days have been spent playing soccer." Said Mia.

"They just cut the grass, and I adore playing soccer on nicely groomed grass. Sophia retorted."

"Sophia, we always follow your lead; now it is my turn to decide," Mia was growing impatient.

Sophia yelled, "Fine, go do whatever you want by yourself. I am playing soccer."

Mia left. She was indignant. She discovered that she still had Sophia's journal when she came home. "So, I am not returning it today," too angry with her, Mia pondered.

Their teacher asked for their notebooks the following day at class. Because she was missing hers, Sophia asked her teacher if she could bring it in the next day. Sophia had taken a favor from her teacher. Sophia returned to her seat while maintaining a troubled expression. Mia was struggling with a personal issue. She was still enraged at Sophia for not making a deal with her the previous day in the park, even though she knew she should have informed her teacher that she had the notebook.

Mia waited to speak with the teacher until it was time for lunch.

"I have Sophia's journal." She told her teacher since Mia, and I disagreed the day before, I should have spoken up sooner.

Could you please assist us in finding a solution? Asked Mia.

"Mia, I appreciate your concern. Sophia will no doubt be grateful that you have given me her notebook. I am delighted you requested assistance in resolving the issue. This is a fantastic approach because resolving a situation on your own is challenging when you are still furious."

Their teacher sat with the girls and spoke at recess.

They both admitted that they frequently found the other person infuriating since they did not always want to do the Williams things, but they later realized that their problems had never really been resolved. One of them simply returned home each day. Their teacher assisted them in realizing that perhaps being best friends did not require them to play together daily.

They decided to limit their playtime to a few times a week and play each game on alternate terms. The disputes Mia and Sophia had recently might finally come to an end.

Your Turn

What was the issue in the friendship of Mia and Sophia?

_____

_____

_____

_____

What did you understand from the story?

_____

_____

_____

_____

_____

_____

What would Mia and Sophia have done to resolve their issue?

_____

_____

_____

_____

How did Mia and Sophia's experiences differ from each other?

_____

_____

_____

_____

What do you think is required to move on from a disagreement and keep your friends close to your heart?

_____

_____

_____

_____

_____

_____

_____

_____

Let's Face It

After hearing the story of Sophia and Mia, think about your friend and ask these questions to understand the warmth of your friendship.

Am I comfortable with myself while being around this friend?

_____

_____

_____

_____

_____

_____

Do we understand each other?

_____

_____

_____

_____

_____

_____

Are We Helpful to each other?

_____

_____

_____

_____

_____

_____

Is it possible for me to be my true self, or do I need to put on a front to keep the friendship alive?

_____

_____

_____

_____

_____

_____

My Promises

Here are some promises you need to make to be a good friend.

I Will Let the Love Grow

Friends are important, but they are not just my friends. I won't stop them from making new friends, and I'll keep the door open to establishing new ones. Meeting new people can bring us many beautiful things without detracting from our relationships with others already in our life. There is never a shortage of love.

I Will Embrace the Change

I'll be there for my friends as they grow. I won't be afraid of them or try to stop them; instead, I'll support them and rejoice in their achievements. I'll accept and welcome the changes in my own life as well.

I Will Be Honest

I'll be open and honest in my communication with my buddies. We shall speak and listen candidly because neither they nor I can read minds. I know that interactions might occasionally be awkward, and that is OK.

I Will Give Them Space

We need our room to be ourselves because my buddies and I are different people. Both my friends and I are entitled to our perspectives and worldviews. The best friendships are the ones that let us be our truest selves.

I Will Put My Efforts

I am aware that everyone makes mistakes. I won't end a friendship over a single issue. We will commit to talking, getting better, and moving on if the friendship is a good relationship overall.

I Will Be Empathetic

My friends and I are both complete; we have all we need. Our decision to be friends enriches and adds value to our lives. For our happiness, we are not reliant on one another. I will still be sympathetic and helpful without fully owning my friend's emotions or problems.

I Will Not Hurt Someone

Because friendship is unique, and I get to pick my friends, not everyone is my friend. Everyone deserves kindness and respect, though. I will never boast about my friendships to put someone else down or hurt them.

Only Love and Care

Love and caring behavior are what my friends deserve. I won't make fun of my friends. I'll also try to confront individuals who mistreat my friends.

I Will Ask for Help

I will always seek assistance if I believe one of my friends needs it or is in danger. My friend might be upset, but their security and well-being come first. Sharing trust is more important. It entails having faith in your friends to guide you in the right direction when issues arise.

Putting it All Together

One of life's greatest pleasures is having a true friend by your side. Finding someone who laughs with you when you are happy, lifts your spirits when you are sad, and always has your back is a great feeling. However, not every friendship is made equal. Your connection could not be healthy if you feel insignificant, depressed, or fearful in their presence. Friendship should uplift your spirits. It should provide you with joy. Disagreements happen, but if you are frequently at odds, you might not get along.

A good friend won't be upset if you hang out with someone else, even if jealousy can happen occasionally. It is crucial to create secure and healthy friendships. Being in an unhealthy friendship is not good for anyone. Speak to a parent or another responsible adult if you believe your friendship may be unhealthy.

Imagine the world as you would like it to be. Practice discussing it with your friend in this manner. Try to make new, different pals as well. Be patient. Finding people, you connect with is not always simple. Find kids who are interested in some of your hobbies. Spend time learning about their personality to determine whether they are sincere, reliable, and nice.

You do not always need a lot of friends. Your life can be significantly brighter with just one or two true friends. What does characterize a good or true friend? Sharing, listening, assisting, and respect are some top qualities. Keeping friends requires some effort. You must be a good friend if you want to have one.

Be respectful and kind to others as you would like to be treated. Tell the truth. Although it is important, to be honest, you can also be kind. Express your emotions. Instead of backbiting or ignoring a buddy with whom you disagree, consider talking to them directly.

Friendship is a two-way street. Encourage your friends and acknowledge their accomplishments. Have fun times with them. Fun times with friends create lasting memories. Children face different issues in making and keeping friends. By reading this book, you have learned what a friend is, how to make sure you are ready to be a good friend, and how to reach a compromise, deal with conflicts, and manage the difficulties of friendships. Enjoy your happy zone with your friends!